Monique Bloise
Renata Santos

The management of basic health units:

Monique Bloise
Renata Santos

The management of basic health units:

Limits, possibilities and challenges within the shared management model

ScienciaScripts

Imprint
Any brand names and product names mentioned in this book are subject to trademark, brand or patent protection and are trademarks or registered trademarks of their respective holders. The use of brand names, product names, common names, trade names, product descriptions etc. even without a particular marking in this work is in no way to be construed to mean that such names may be regarded as unrestricted in respect of trademark and brand protection legislation and could thus be used by anyone.

Cover image: www.ingimage.com

This book is a translation from the original published under ISBN 978-3-330-76484-2.

Publisher:
Sciencia Scripts
is a trademark of
Dodo Books Indian Ocean Ltd. and OmniScriptum S.R.L publishing group

120 High Road, East Finchley, London, N2 9ED, United Kingdom
Str. Armeneasca 28/1, office 1, Chisinau MD-2012, Republic of Moldova, Europe
Managing Directors: Ieva Konstantinova, Victoria Ursu
info@omniscriptum.com

Printed at: see last page
ISBN: 978-620-8-50315-4

I dedicate this book to my mother (in memoriam) who constantly guides me, my star and source of inspiration. The light that strengthens me. Many thanks for all her teachings.

Listen to the sounds of nature and, in the same way, listen to people. Listen without attaching anything to what you're listening to - don't judge, because the moment you judge, the listening stops. Whenever there are alternatives, be careful. Don't opt for the convenient, the comfortable, the respectable, the socially acceptable, the honourable. Choose what makes your heart flutter. Choose what you would like to do, despite all the (onsHquèncias" **(OSHO).**

Summary

Presentation

The motivation to carry out this study began with the restlessness I developed during my professional experience as manager of a Basic Health Unit (UBS), where I experienced the anguish and dilemmas of exercising this function.

As well as technical and bureaucratic issues, the work process also included mediating conflicts, organising and monitoring the work of the family health teams, knowing and using information systems, creating spaces for continuing education, listening in a qualified manner, meeting management demands, liaising with the social facilities in the area and, above all, carrying out these functions with leadership and balance.

In the course of this journey, questions arose about the work of the UBS manager: Which professional would be capable of working in such a diverse universe? Would they be prepared to respond to so many demands? What competences are needed to fulfil this role?

This gave rise to an interest in studying the profile of this professional, who is considered an important part of the family health work process, seeking to promote quality, efficiency and effectiveness in the health actions offered to the population.

So I embarked on a quest to learn more about this professional's work process, as well as the limits, challenges and possibilities of carrying out this role. Based on this knowledge, I wanted to reflect on the tools needed to enhance the work of management in primary healthcare.

Monique Bloise

Introduction

The implementation of the Unified Health System (SUS) in the 1990s brought about a major change in the structure and organisation of health services in Brazil, in that its basic principles are: universality, comprehensiveness, equity, decentralisation and social control. In practice, this fundamentally means access to health services at all levels of care for all Brazilian citizens, enabling social participation in the definition, monitoring and implementation of health policies in a process of co-responsibility between the three spheres of government (ESCOREL et al, 2008).

This new model of care sees Primary Health Care (PHC) as the gateway and structuring axis of the health system. This model was strengthened with the implementation of the Family Health Programme in 1994, which evolved into a more comprehensive and integrative approach through the Family Health Strategy (ESF), starting in 2006 (BRASIL, 1998/2006).

In order to characterise this trajectory, it is interesting to recall the construction of the Pact for Health, which since 2003, through discussions between the National Council of Health Secretaries (CONASS) and the Ministry of Health (MS), has encouraged revisions to the normative processes established for the SUS, in order to take into account the diversities of the country, under the aegis of health responsibility, adapted to the reality of each state (MACHADO et al, 2009).

The Pact for Health is a set of institutional reforms of the SUS agreed between the three spheres of management - the Union, States and Municipalities. The Pact for Health is implemented by means of these three spheres signing up to the Management Commitment Agreement (TCG), which is renewed annually with the establishment of targets and commitments for each entity. Its aim is to promote the improvement of the services offered and guarantee access to the entire population with quality and efficiency (BRASIL, 2006).

Through the Pact for Life and the National Primary Care Policy (PNAB - Ordinance GM 648/2006), the Family Health Strategy has been consolidated as a priority action for strengthening and reorganising PHC in Brazil. As a result, the ESF has been expanded to large urban centres, through a set of health actions, both individual and collective, covering health promotion, disease prevention, treatment, rehabilitation and health maintenance (BRASIL, 2006).

The Family Health Strategy as a model of care to reorient primary care is considered the main gateway and the centre of communication with the Health Care Network. It is therefore essential that it is guided by the principles of universality, accessibility, linkage, continuity of care, comprehensive care, accountability, humanisation, equity and social participation (BRASIL, 2006).

In order for the health actions offered by all levels of care to be effective, it is essential to organise the services into a network, so that there is a synergistic connection between them, allowing care to be coordinated in an integrated and effective way. For this to happen, there must be good communication between all the actors involved in the management of PHC services, organising them democratically, with a view to giving local managers greater autonomy.

The primary level is important in the coordination of care and articulation of the network, needing expanded technical knowledge and the development of skills in solving problems and/or directing users to other levels of care, such as the secondary and tertiary levels.

In this sense, health management brings new challenges from the perspective of network organisation, provoking community involvement in the process of building health to the implementation of new management models, considering social participation, user satisfaction, professional qualification and investment in improvements in working conditions, in order to promote greater resoluteness in the health actions developed (GONÇALVES, BARBOSA and SOUZA, 2012).

With the management of primary care in mind, Municipal Law No. 5026, approved on 19 May 2009 in the municipality of Rio de Janeiro, regulated the work of Social Health Organisations (OSS) with specific rules for the health sector, which enabled the Municipal Health Secretariat (SMS) to inaugurate a shared management model guided by management contracts, with the aim of promoting greater agility in the conduct of actions and in the administration of health services.

The implementation of this new management model prioritised and had PHC at its core, expanding and consolidating in the municipality of Rio de Janeiro from 2009 onwards, against a backdrop of political and administrative reform, the guidelines of which refer to the Master Plan for Reform of the State Apparatus (PDRAE, 1995), which indicated as a strategy that public services would no longer be managed directly by the state, but by non-governmental entities in the public interest, whose actions would be regulated and supervised by the state.

In this context, the institutionalisation of the outsourcing of health services was fostered with the drafting of the OSS bill, which allowed for the "publicisation" of these non-state-exclusive services, i.e. their transfer from the state sector to the non-state public sector. According to the PDRAE (1995), the main objective of this OSS project was to deliberate on the decentralisation process, where health services would no longer be under the direct power of the state, considering that the OSS would make the processes and services they administer more dynamic.

From the perspective of this new management model, the state defines the guidelines for the management, monitoring and inspection of the execution of the duties recommended for the OSS under contract, and the OSS are responsible for carrying out the contractual activities and duties, as well as rendering accounts and providing assistance and management results defined in a "Management Contract".

Through the management contract, the actions and services that were previously the responsibility of the state are transferred to the OSS, which become the executors of the policy. To this end, the civil organisations were given managerial autonomy to hire human resources and purchase movable and immovable property without a bidding process, giving them the autonomy to manage, execute and provide public health services (REZENDE, 2004).

In this context, the manager is responsible for managing the UBS, organising health services, monitoring the actions of the family health teams and carrying out technical-bureaucratic activities in this setting. They are also responsible for ensuring that the principles, policies and guidelines that guide health actions in the ESF in the SUS model are complied with, promoting the qualification of work and workers, as well as meeting the demands and needs of the population.

Managers' daily lives are therefore marked by the challenge of guaranteeing clinical governance based on the policies and guidelines of the SMS, to whom they must be accountable, and administrative management based on the fulfilment of targets agreed between the SMS and the OSS, to whom these managers are also accountable.

From this perspective, Campos (2003) considers institutional support to be an important way of strengthening and legitimising relationships between individuals, knowing that management does not exist without this aspect, even if the actors represent different levels of knowledge and power. Without recognising that management only exists in interaction with others, there is a risk of reproducing bureaucratised and impoverished processes at work.

From this perspective, the Paideia method sees management as transforming the way workers and users are and act, and through certain methodological resources it allows this encounter to be dealt with in a particular way. In other words, the differences in roles, power and knowledge are recognised, even though the aim is to establish constructive relationships between the different social actors.

For Campos (2006) "Paideia is therefore a methodology for educating people with the aim of expanding their capacity to analyse and intervene in the world. It is not a neutral technique; the suggested method is based on certain values and criteria to guide policy and management."

It is therefore understood that institutional support articulates common knowledge, desires and objectives in order to strengthen the relationship between workers and users, supporting and at the same time pushing the other, considering that pressure from the outside implies bringing something external to the group that conducts the work and its implications for work processes. "Those who ***are supportive support and, at the same time, push the other, while also being costly. Cudo junto C CO cesMO CA^O"*** (CAMPOS, 2003).

he inherent complexity of the health field, with cross-flows, unpredictable situations that generate unexpected problems that cannot be solved simply through prior knowledge or standardised techniques. In this way, the manager represents a strategic link in the organisation of work and the production of learning, being able to critically mobilise available resources to solve problems (FRANCO, SANTOS and SALGADO, 2011).

Therefore, the great challenge for policy makers, managers and researchers in the field of health work management would be to develop governance models that are capable of integrating the clinical and administrative dimensions of management, so that the desired results are not just quantitative, but also include the efficiency, quality and effectiveness of the actions developed. Theory must be intertwined with practice, i.e. it must function not just as a means of providing knowledge, but must be capable of provoking reflections that help resolve conflicts, transforming reality and mobilising professionals to achieve a common goal (FRANCO, SANTOS and SALGADO, 2011).

According to Silva (2012), knowing the problems and social relevance of health service management is extremely important in order to encourage discussions to explore ways of achieving quality management based on the guidelines and principles of the SUS.

In this context, some questions arise: What profile of manager is working in the UBS in the municipality of RJ? What are the predominant work activities of health unit managers in the municipality of Rio de Janeiro? What are the main problems, potentialities and challenges identified in the exercise of this function?

Based on these questions, the aim of this study was to analyse the limits, possibilities and challenges related to the work of UBS managers in a context of shared management between the state and social organisations, seeking to identify tools to enhance the work of these professionals in the institutional and clinical governance dimensions.

The specific objectives were: to characterise the profile of managers; to investigate the work of managers in the new model of care and management of social organisations in the municipality of Rio de Janeiro; to analyse the work of managers from the perspective of administrative actions and clinical governance; to identify the potential, weaknesses and challenges of the work of managers in the management model adopted by the SMS.

CHAPTER 1

Contextualisation

The global economic crisis in the 1970s led to an intensification of reformist ideas to redefine the role of the state and its scope for action, as the current interventionist and bureaucratic model began to be questioned. This led to greater concern in capitalist countries about advances in public sector performance, which, associated with the economic crisis attributed to the welfare state, led to the ideals of state reform (RODRIGUES, 2007).

From a neoliberal perspective, the role and efficiency of the state were being strongly questioned and the alternatives for tackling this scenario involved rationalising resources and stripping the power of institutions that were considered unproductive in the logic of the market.

It was in this context of crisis that the discussion about a Third Way emerged in England as a counterpoint to the neoliberal model of the time. According to Giddens (2001), ***the*** Third Way attempts to unite a "half-theory" of neoliberal economic efficiency ***with*** another ***"half-theory"*** of social justice, linked to the traditional left (formerly social democracy), recognising that both are necessary for a decent economy and a just society.

Also according to according to the author, for the Third Way, and more recently for the new developmentalism, the basis of the crisis would also be inefficiency. The alternative to dealing with this crisis would be to reform the state, in order to make it more efficient, not by opening it up to the market, but by involving the third sector, represented by non-profit institutions and organised civil society, based on the principle that those who profit from social goods should use them responsibly and give something back to the community (GIDDENS, 2001). give something back to the community (GIDDENS, 2001).

The participation of organised civil society is seen as a characteristic of citizenship, a maxim that should be applied to politicians and citizens, the poor and the rich, companies and individuals. This new current is strengthened by the social democracy model and influences reforms in public administration, with the managerialist model as its centrepiece (GIDDENS, 2001).

In this context of reform and exhaustion of the bureaucratic model, which led to inefficiency related to excessive procedures and processes, the concept of new public management emerged (GRAU, 2000). In addition to a low commitment to the political system and the needs of society, the new public management sought to make public administration more flexible and increase government accountability, promoting greater control, efficiency and effectiveness of results in sectors previously run by direct administration (Pinho and Sacramento 2009).

In Brazil, the 1980s were marked by two important movements: the first was influenced by socialist ideology, which can be identified in social movements. The first was influenced by socialist ideology, which can be identified in the social movements. This movement brought the issue of defending citizenship with the participation of civil society in decision-making in relation to public policies, allied to the re-democratisation of the country; and the second was based on the new managerialist model for public administration with the Reform of the State.

Inserted in an international economic context of transformation, with political guidelines for opening up the market, shrinking the state and privatising government companies, the reform proposal represents the need to reshape the state and establish new forms of relationship with civil society, assigning it new roles in economic and social processes. This configuration of the state-society relationship, given its relevance and magnitude, has been the focus of debate on government policies, especially in the social area, in the mainstream media and in influential segments of national political, financial and business thinking. This process of remodelling the Brazilian state, which began in the 1980s, really came to fruition under the Fernando Henrique Cardoso government in 1995, with the Administrative Reform proposal presented by then Minister Bresser Pereira (Pinho and Sacramento 2009).

Breaking away from bureaucratic public administration was not a recent plan, since Decree-Law 200 of 25 February 1967 started the debate on state reform with principles of administrative rationality and managerial efficiency. These principles were also pursued in the National Debureaucratisation Programme, created in the early 1980s to combat the current bureaucratic structure (PINTO, 2001).

The 1988 Constitution aimed to guarantee social protection as a direct action by the state, but through Constitutional Amendment no. 19, of 4 June 1998, the principle of efficiency became part of the heading of art. 37, guiding the Brazilian Public Administration with government directives to implement the managerial model, inducing the "Administrative Reform" that had been interrupted in the 1988 Constitution (PINTO, 2001).

> "Reforming the state apparatus means guaranteeing it greater governance, i.e. greater capacity to govern, greater ability to implement laws and public policies. It means making exclusive state activities much more efficient by transforming local authorities into 'autonomous agencies', and also making competitive social services much more efficient by transforming them into non-state public organisations of a special kind: 'social organisations'" (PDRAE, p. 44-45).

According to Costa e Silva (2014), the changes that began in 1995 marked the transition from the state promoting economic and social development to the state regulating that development . In this sense, state action in the execution or direct provision of services considered to be non-exclusive to the state would be reduced, thus enhancing its regulatory function. This process would encourage a competitive contractual model, which would increase the state's capacity to implement public policies efficiently.

As a result, the Reform of the State was shaped around three basic, complementary and interdependent strategic dimensions: institutional-legal: reform of the legal system and property relations; cultural: transition from a bureaucratic culture to a managerial culture, and managerial: modernisation of the current bureaucratic administration and introduction of managerial administration (COSTA and SILVA, 2014).

According to Martins (2006), Managerial Public Administration has some characteristics, such as:

> "Strategic or result-oriented nature of the decision-making process; b) decentralisation; c) flexibility; d) increasing performance and payment for performance/productivity; e) internal and external competitiveness; f) strategic direction; g) transparency and accountability; h) differentiated patterns of delegation and decision-making discretion; i) separation of policy from its management; j) development of managerial skills; k) outsourcing; l) limitation of the stability of civil servants and temporary employment regimes; and m) differentiated structures" (MARTINS, 2006, p. 21).21).

From this perspective, publicisation would make it possible for the non-state public sector to produce competitive services, establishing a system of partnership between the state and society for its financing and control, in which debureaucratisation, management autonomy, efficiency and results-orientation based on management contracts with non-state public entities would make it possible to create a new institutional design for public administration (BRASIL, 1995).

As a reform proposal, a draft law and decree regulating social organisations (OS) was drawn up. In 1997, Provisional Measure 1591 determined that these entities, once authorised, would be able to partner with the state in the running of public affairs. And finally, with Law 9.637/1998, the OS were established, along with management contracts and the National Publicisation Programme.

From the government's point of view, the SOs would improve management performance, enabling greater flexibility in the provision of public services, without administrative ties to the state, but fostered with public funds and controlled by management contracts. In this way, the state acts more as a regulator and promoter of public services and the OS stimulate decentralisation, de-bureaucratisation, autonomy and quality of management, favouring more dynamic management of the health sector and an increase in the capacity to plan and carry out actions through targets agreed in management contracts and evaluated by the responsible bodies (ABRUCIO and SANO, 2008).

The transfer of state responsibilities through the outsourcing of services and the establishment of management contracts with Law 9637/1998 generated a series of demonstrations and reactions against the new model, mainly by the Health Councils and Conferences of the time. In Rio de Janeiro, Roraima and the Federal District, the Public Prosecutor's Office even filed a public civil action against this type of outsourcing.

These actions against the new management model reduced the strength of its expansion over the years. Thus, initially, the expansion of this model on a large scale was halted, and it was not possible to implement it nationwide as had been planned with the State Reform (REZENDE, 2004).

On the other hand, with the aim of creating alternatives to the serious gaps in the provision of public services and infrastructure in a wide range of sectors such as health, education, sanitation, the environment, employment and income, there has been a growth in the Third Sector or non-state public sector since the country's re-democratisation in the 1980s (RODRIGUES, 2007).

In the Municipality of Rio de Janeiro, the choice to work with this management model was institutionalised through Municipal Law No. 5026, approved on 19 May 2009, enacted on the basis of Decree-Law 30.780 of 2 June 2009. In this law, the Municipality of Rio de Janeiro regulates the work of Social Organisations with specific rules for the health sector. From then on, through management contracts, the Municipal Health Department of Rio de Janeiro (SMS/RJ) and the OSs inaugurated a shared management model, with the aim of promoting greater agility in the conduct of actions and in the administration of health services.

According to Lima and Rivera (2012), contractualisation has been increasingly used in various countries between government health authorities and private or state providers of primary and hospital care, with the aim of improving the performance of providers and the accountability of results for the various players (users, funders and governments). For these authors, ***"the underlying assumption*** is that unsatisfactory results are partly determined by insufficient accountability and the transfer of financial resources that is not conditional on ***performance".***

The state's control over the OS is based on monitoring the targets previously agreed in the management contract and the results obtained by the organisation. These results are monitored by the Technical Evaluation Commission (CTA), which is under the responsibility of the supervising body or organisation and whose members are appointed by the same body.

For Escoval, Silva and Hortale (2014), who carried out a study on the experience of Portugal and Brazil in contractualisation in Primary Health Care, contractualisation is a complex process that requires the reorganisation of services and the existence of robust information systems in order to carry out certain actions such as surveying needs, priorities, verifying installed capacity, negotiating, establishing indicators and targets, monitoring, evaluating and applying incentives, as well as penalties. All these procedures become even more difficult considering the subjective dimension of health care, and the achievement of results cannot be seen in a standardised way to the detriment of the peculiarities of each territory and the ways in which health is produced.

All the difficulties that exist in the complexity of this process need to be recognised, at the risk of contractualisation becoming disconnected from its main objective and from performance evaluation, becoming a mere bureaucratic instrument for charging and meeting targets, reducing its transformative character and leading to the establishment of strictly hierarchical control management (ESCOVAL, SILVA AND HORTALE, 2014).

Also according to Escoval, Silva and Hortale (2014), in relation to the management contract, there is a set of monitoring indicators and a system of incentives that need constant review and adjustment. Although contractualisation is a results management strategy, these indicators are more related to processes than results, i.e. they depend on installed capacity, care provision, economic performance and efficiency.

In this sense, we are left to reflect on the fact that low targets would not reward good health results, and very high targets would cause professional discouragement or even focus only on certain practices. Therefore, the ideal result would be to achieve a balance between these two aspects (ESCOVAL, SILVA AND HORTALE 2014).

CHAPTER 2

Theoretical Framework

The conceptual framework of this research is based on three axes: the new management model through Social Organisations, the management of health work in Primary Care and the management of care. By bringing together these three major themes, which refer us to the concepts of clinical governance, the managerial function in UBS and work in PHC, we sought to create a frame of reference that would help us analyse the reality of work and managerial activity and reflect on possibilities for improving the model.

The new management model through Social Organisations

As mentioned above, the term "managerialism" was introduced into public administration in the context of discussions about the Third Way and the need to increase the state's managerial capacity and resolutiveness. In Brazil, this discussion gained weight with the proposal for Administrative Reform under the Fernando Henrique Cardoso government and was expressed in the adoption of new management mechanisms in public administration, including the contractualisation of health services.

Against the backdrop of this new management model adopted by the state and, in this specific study, by the Municipality of Rio de Janeiro, it became important to look for a theoretical framework that addressed the issue of management from a perspective that was not only political, but also in the field of administration, in order to understand how the operationalisation of contractualised services has been taking place, as well as its difficulties and possibilities.

The following is a literature review on the managerial function and its specificity in the field of health in order to provide elements that allow us to understand and dialogue with the daily life and practice of UBS managers in a context of shared management between the State and Social Organisations.

The Basic Operational Standard (NOB-SUS 01/1996) made a distinction between management and administration, in which management is the responsibility for running a health system in the different spheres of government, at federal, state and municipal level, exercising functions of coordination, articulation, planning, negotiation, monitoring, control, evaluation and auditing. Management would be the administration of a health unit or body - outpatient clinic, hospital, institute, foundation, among others, characterised as providing services to the system.

Even with this conceptual distinction, there is still no clear definition of the role and attributions of managers in health units and services. This creates difficulties in really understanding the functions and work of these professionals, leading to an excessive absorption of activities and compromising effectiveness and management in health production, clinical governance and the quality of health services offered to users (XIMENES NETO and SAMPAIO, 2007).

The emergence of management in health services has led to a rethinking of the administrative practices that had already been used in the health sector. An effective organisation requires competent work focused on controlling financial, human and material resources and on organisational objectives. In this sense, management must be committed to meeting these objectives, mediating between people, technologies, materials and the environment (JUNQUEIRA, 1990).

> "Management is the most important administrative function - it is the process of making decisions that affect the structure, production processes and product of a system. It involves coordinating the efforts of the various parts of that system, controlling the processes and performance of the parts and evaluating the final products and results. In an organisation, the manager is responsible for the effective and efficient use of inputs in order to translate them into products (services, for example) that lead the organisation to achieve the results expected of it." (TANCREDI, 1998 apud PASSOS e CIOSAK, p.2, 2006).

The adoption of flexible management models and the guarantee of popular participation are crucial strategies in the current policy to strengthen the health system. The technical and managerial reorganisation of services requires a transformation of health actions and the involvement of professionals with services and users, in order to provide greater resolution and quality in health actions (GUIMARÃES and ÉVORA, 2004).

Loch (2009) in his thesis on the experience of ESF doctors when they took over the management of UBS highlights the work of Drucker (1967), an influential personality in modern administration who, after the Second World War, in his book The Effective Manager, discusses the concept of the manager from a viewpoint related to communication and leadership and the ability to influence the organisation's decisions. Drucker states that in addition to knowledge and efficiency, the manager must be effective and, to achieve this, follow some basic guidelines, such as: time control; striving for results by focusing on the external contribution; building based on the strengths of the organisation and the players involved, i.e. based on what can be done and not on their weaknesses; choosing priorities that will produce excellent results; effective decisions based on divergent opinions and not on the appreciation of facts.

Loch (2009) also mentions an article by Ducker, published in 2004 in the Havard Business

Review, which proposes eight practices for effective managers. Managers should: ask what needs to be done; ask what is good for the company; make action plans; take responsibility for the decision; take responsibility for communication; focus on opportunities rather than problems; hold productive meetings and speak "we" rather than "I".

In the health sector, the professional who manages a UBS must be prepared to: deal with unexpected events that can happen to users in the UBS or at home; relate to the extended interprofessional teams; be aware of medical care procedures, as well as mediating possible conflicts in inter-relational situations (GRIGOLETTO and RAMOS, 2012).

The manager has the role of exercising and developing leadership in relation to family health teams, transforming ideas, intentions and goals into results, harmonising the working environment for professionals, actively participating in planning processes, knowing the guidelines of the SUS and the Family Health Strategy in order to meet the demands and needs of the population (GRIGOLETTO and RAMOS, 2012).

In addition, managers need to be qualified, recognising the most important instruments and tools for their work, enabling them to identify potential and optimise the work of the team, creating new leaders in order to exercise shared management, setting an example of conduct for efficient work that constantly improves its quality (FRANCO, SANTOS and SALGADO, 2011).

These arguments support the study by Motta (1996), who states that the managerial function is full of dualities with many routines and techniques that undergo different interventions, presenting a flexibility that characterises work in a fragmented and intermittent way.

Therefore, democratic management requires that the manager has the ability to mobilise his team based on the planning of priority actions identified in the territory under his responsibility, being able to strategically tackle new problems that may arise (DUSSAULT, 1992).

Working with a multi-professional team requires knowledge of the role of each professional in the team so that decision-making can be shared ethically, meeting the needs of users in the production of care and the emancipation of all the actors involved (DUSSAULT, 1992).

It is also important for the manager to be able to identify the strengths and weaknesses of each professional in their team, guaranteeing continuous improvement to enable them to deal with the complexities and challenges of a job influenced by social, economic and epidemiological variables in a territory that is constantly changing.

According to Mintzberg (2007), managers face great difficulties, as they are overloaded with obligations that they often can't delegate, suffer pressure and have the responsibility of frequently planning and rescheduling their working day. This professional is in charge of the entire organisation and is the formal authority that deals with various interpersonal relationships, through which they mobilise information to be used in decision-making. These conditions mean that these professionals fulfil interpersonal, informational and decision-making functions.

The frustrations faced by managers are related to the vulnerability to which people who are in power and have not yet developed the ability to deal with these situations are exposed. However, this can be reversed if the professional maintains a balance between personality and action in the organisation, in order to achieve professional growth and quality in their actions (ZALEZNIK, 1993; STEWART, 1982).

For Franco, Santos and Salgado (2011), the manager is recognised as a professional who mobilises and organises the means for the organisation to fulfil its purpose, working where work processes, people and plans often clash, as there is external pressure for agility and flexibility, while at the same time there is a growing internal need for control and predictability.

Faced with the complex arrangement for guaranteeing the quality of the health services offered, challenges are created for local management that would lie on the boundaries between the freedom of the worker and their commitment to the health network.

In this context, it is interesting to recall the study by Maffei (2011), where some questions were raised:

> "How can we combine institutional democratisation with operational capacity and, therefore, with some degree of vertical centralisation, without which establishments would get lost in endless discussions or particularisms? How can we provide independence and autonomy for each team, without losing the sense of a network of commitments, without losing the notion of a system, or without compromising the guideline of comprehensive care? How can we ensure a dialogue between users and professionals? How can we reduce some of the alienation and bureaucratisation typical of managerial work? How can we motivate professionals and increase their capacity for reflection and self-esteem? How can autonomy and creativity be combined with professional responsibility? (MAFFEI,2011, p.35)".

In view of this, psychic mobilisation, financial objectives and the production of adherence to work are important characteristics in the subjective and affective involvement of managers with the organisation. Work becomes the embodiment of each individual's desires, considering the desire for success, new challenges, the need for recognition and reward for personal merit. It is a place of self-fulfilment, where work can generate concrete products, making it possible to assess quality based on well-established criteria, knowing that the subjectivities of the players have a direct impact on the meaning of the action (GAULEJAC, 2007).

In this way, carrying out management activities requires the use of interdisciplinary tools, taking into account technical capacity, but also the ability to articulate the political-economic-social relations that exist in the work process (VANDERLEI and ALMEIDA 2007).

According to Junqueira and Inojosa (1992), a managerial practice committed to collective health and guaranteeing quality health services to users makes it possible to change perspective and act in a more comprehensive and participatory way, thus moving closer to the interests of society and a state project built collectively with well-defined responsibilities for each actor involved in health production.

Thus, promoting transformations in this field does not depend on training in how to be a manager. It is necessary to identify, develop and improve technical and administrative skills, but above all, a managerial practice of leadership, commitment, autonomy and organisational flexibility. An important tool for the success of this process is information. Managers who are able to assimilate, share and use information, transferring it in an interactive and strategic way, lead their work in a dynamic way, improving the quality of health services for the population and, consequently, guaranteeing work guided by good health practices (FRANCO, SANTOS and SALGADO, 2011).

For Ciampone and André (2007) it is clear that managers still act along the lines of traditional administrative principles, where planning is done in a bureaucratic and fragmented way. What's more, the ideas and thoughts expressed and listed in managers' representations are not always implemented in their practices, creating a distancing in this professional's way of thinking and acting, which directly influences the operationalisation of health action strategies and consequently the efficiency and effectiveness of these actions.

A powerful differentiator between the bureaucratic process and more flexible management is the creation of bonds and the recognition of health production and results as the end activity of managerial work. To do this, management needs to organise its work using the necessary tools so that the expected results can be achieved together with the health teams (FRANCO, SANTOS and SALGADO, 2011).

Managers need to be prepared to deal with challenges such as conflict mediation, management of production processes in the health field, work management with a focus on quality of user care, as well as meeting the three dimensions of work. The political dimension, which relates to the purpose of the work; the organisational dimension, which induces the organisation of the management process; and the technical dimension, which relates to the practice of this work (FRANCO, SANTOS and SALGADO, 2011).

Reinforcing this discussion, Dussault (1992) states that this "***is a management that recognises the central role of professionals and, at the same time, has mechanisms to avoid the unwanted effects of the autonomy of professional practice and*** corporatism. This management emphasises the definition of decision-making mechanisms that involve professionals both in the formulation of objectives and general guidelines and in the evaluation of results: this management accepts that ***professionals work***

not because they obey orders, but out of responsibility".

All the guidelines for effective management work are immersed in an unpredictable reality in which any decision taken implies staying with or changing established processes. This constant transformation requires a leader and autonomous manager. This autonomy also needs to be stimulated in staff and users of health services, changing states of consciousness towards a more autonomous and participatory management and production of health. The autonomous manager needs to prioritise their actions and delegate functions. As a result, the organisation of work becomes more meaningful and favours better health outcomes.

Most of the specialisation and management training courses that exist in Brazil are still very much focused on hospital administration. The thinkers and planners of these courses have given little thought to UBS management projects, with activities related to family health teams in which prevention and health promotion are the focus of the professionals' work. The activities should not only take into account the reorganisation of services, but also local specificities and the aspects inherent in a flexible management practice (FERREIRA, 2004).

In an effort to meet this demand, the creation of an undergraduate programme in public health has led to reflection on the training of public health professionals. Unlike other courses in the health area, which don't always include aspects of public health in their curricula, graduates seek postgraduate courses to complement their knowledge in the area of public health. Professionals graduating in Public Health broaden their knowledge of health determinants, management models and health care models (ENSP/FIOCRUZ, 2015).

The sanitarian, as a new professional entering the labour market, brings knowledge within a broader paradigm in the area of health, as well as the interdisciplinarity and political character needed to face the current challenges in the field of public health, considering that the focus of these professionals' work is in the area of politics, management and planning in the running of health services (ANJOS and PINTO).

According to Abrasco's final report on undergraduate studies in Collective Health, the Sanitarian's knowledge covers complex fields ranging from the health-disease process, the formulation and implementation of intersectoral public policies and the implementation of actions within health services and social organisations. The structuring axes of this course include the areas of Epidemiology, Management and Planning, Health Surveillance and Health Promotion (ABRASCO, 2009).

In view of this, the sanitarian becomes a strategic professional who would be able to act in an expanded way from the perspective of the new management model and new care model, with mastery in the area of public policies, health planning, health surveillance, among others of extreme importance for the management of UBS within the principles of the SUS and ESF guidelines.

According to Loch (2009), the position of UBS manager is fraught with personal suffering, high energy consumption, unsatisfactory performance, high turnover in management positions and a high level of job abandonment. Even with the difficulties related to this position, most of the existing qualification courses focus on the organisational and functional issues of the Unified Health System (SUS), i.e. subjective, relational, clinical management and people management issues are rarely addressed in the spaces where these professionals are discussed and trained.

Health work management in primary care

The contractualisation that took place in the city of Rio de Janeiro was set up with little participation and autonomy on the part of local management health professionals. Despite the teams' incipient participation, the introduction of the incentive system was seen as an inducement to achieve the desired results and as a stimulus to reflect on the work process and improve the planning of health actions.

Therefore, this model of shared management in PHC has led to a process of negotiation with the aim of ensuring planning, accountability of units and teams with a certain amount of autonomy, a contribution to the coordination of health organisations and, consequently, an improvement in their performance and health outcomes (COSTA and SILVA, 2014).

As a result, the transfer of responsibilities from the state to the OS through contractualisation delegated to third parties the responsibility for: hiring employees without a public tender, purchasing goods and services without a bidding process, which would result in better services for the community, greater managerial autonomy, lower costs and increased efficiency in health services (REZENDE, 2004).

In this sense, greater emphasis could be placed on negotiation through internal contractualisation , which is a possibility for self-management and mutual adjustment in the real movement of healthcare, in a gradual process of consolidation and learning that would require complex managerial skills. This process was considered difficult insofar as concepts such as "needs", "installed capacity", "setting objectives" and "results" are intangible in the subjective conception of health care.

In this way, the creation of the position of UBS manager was important given the complexity of the work in the Family Health Strategy. This position was not initially planned for the structuring of the management model in the units. However, after meetings with representatives of the Social Organisations and the Municipal Health Department, it was agreed that the UBS would have a manager to take care of administrative and technical tasks. A professional with the technical and administrative capacity and specific skills to lead and monitor the teams' work process, as well as the health services offered, would be responsible for seeking the best health results with the least possible expenditure of resources (MAFFEI, 2011).

This configuration generates a number of conflicts in the work activity at local level, since it is in this space that the contradiction generated by different logics and references occurs: health results with quality and social participation versus the fulfilment of targets agreed a priori between contractors and contracted parties (RAMIRES, LOURENÇÃO and SANTOS, 2004).

Overcoming the old administrative processes, which were limited to resolving issues relating to material and human resources and physical structure, has become a more complex process requiring professionals with a good capacity for analysis, action, improvement of practices and determination to achieve results. As well as leadership skills to deal with the changes and challenges that are part of everyday work (RAMIRES, LOURENÇÃO and SANTOS, 2004).

In order to comply with the guidelines of the new model of care structured on the basis of the ESF, management must fully exercise competent leadership so that it can mobilise processes, will and organisational strategies. With the aim of expanding the areas of influence of health work, achieving the targets set by municipal health management and complying with the provisions of the Municipal Health Plan and Law No. 8.080/1990.

The quality of a health service is a task that falls to each of the actors in that service, and to all of them at the same time. To manage is to operate with the game of disputes between these different actors rather than looking for unfulfilled functionality, developing interventions that make it possible to "publicise" the processes of dispute between the actors and the institution and reveal the "contractuality" that they establish between themselves (MERHY and ONOCKO, 1997).

Even those professionals who are committed and qualified to manage health units are not using support instruments and management tools to help them with their work. In view of this, it is important to find out what these professionals need in order to exercise management with quality and so that effective strategies can be devised to qualify management work in the UBS.

The study by Ohira, Junior and Nunes (2014), which aimed to characterise the profile of PHC managers in 49 small municipalities in Paraná, showed a lack of professionalisation, training and institutionalisation of the position in order to perform the managerial role. In addition, the author mentions that management requires competences and tools that constitute a body of knowledge for managing care and tackling problems related to health production. The shortage of qualified professionals means that this actor takes on multiple functions inherent to the work process at the UBS and not just those pertaining to the position of manager.

In the study by Vanderlei (2007), which investigated the practice of ESF managers, the main difficulties in relation to the work of managers were related to the lack of material resources, infrastructure, medicines and human resources, generating impotence and individual responsibility with a sense of isolation on the part of these professionals.

The analysis of the work process revealed a more bureaucratic professional practice, based on hard technologies, geared towards Taylorist administration, with a focus on productivity, but with gaps in relation to humanisation and the user as the centre of care and health production. These difficulties, combined with other complexities such as power disputes and the inhibition of professional autonomy, hinder a more humanised practice, leading to a hegemonic managerial rationality (VANDERLEI, 2007).

The existing literature is more concerned with issues related to laws and norms developed politically, distancing itself from the problems originally posed and the situations inherent in the daily lives of professionals. As a result, there is a risk that aspects that have a direct impact on the quality and organisation of the health services offered will not be valued (VANDERLEI, 2007).

Care Management/Clinical Governance

The work of the ESF is centred on a multi-professional team made up of a doctor, a nurse, a nursing technician and about six community health workers, with the possibility of adding oral health professionals as part of the multi-professional team. Each family health team should be responsible for a maximum of 4,000 people, with the recommended average being 3,000, respecting equity criteria for this definition (BRASIL, 2011).

According to Franco and Júnior (2003), the substitutive nature of the ESF aims to change conventional practices, making health surveillance the centrepiece of care. To achieve this, integrality and hierarchisation require an organised network of services in order to guarantee comprehensive care for individuals and their families. In addition to these principles, the link, territorialisation, home visits, longitudinality, access and coordination of care are essential for providing quality health services and care.

Comprehensiveness is an important device for producing and transforming health care and is directly related to changes in the care model. It is important for health professionals to be familiar with this device in order to rethink their practices, considering all the determinants of health and all the actors involved in this process of co-responsibility and collective construction of care (BRASIL, 2011).

As the territory of the ESF is a dynamic space of disputes, political movements and competing powers, it is necessary to have management with democratic leadership, political flexibility, competence in primary care and in the management of the SUS, where the strengthening of local management is fundamental for the provision of quality health services (BRASIL, 2007).

For good clinical practice to be consolidated as part of the work process of health professionals, planning and leadership are needed in order to reduce the risks of unsuccessful health care. Above all, ensuring the quality of all the processes involved in the effectiveness of health actions must be configured within the logic of clinical governance (ROLAND and BAKER, 1999).

Clinical governance is gaining importance within the orientation of a new organisational model, where user safety and continuous quality improvement are part of an intrinsic and routine culture in all health services. It requires a position of leadership at all points in the health production process, user participation, effective internal communication, valuing education and research, feedback on the performance of professionals involved in health care, rational use of information and systematic learning about good and bad clinical practices (ZWANENGERG and HARRISON, 2009).

Clinical governance is also aligned with the following principles: practice based on access to clinical evidence, adequate infrastructure, systematically shared good practices and innovations, continuous quality improvement processes, data and information monitoring, risk and adverse event reduction programmes, early recognition and treatment of poor clinical performance, leadership development and effective teamwork (ZWANENGERG and HARRISON, 2009).

Care management brings together service micro-management tools, defined locally on the basis of the health determinants identified in the territory. One of these tools is case management, where the health professional responsible seeks to provide quality care involving the user who has needs, in the planning, monitoring and evaluation of health actions. Another very important tool in clinic management is health condition management, defined according to Almeida (2014), p.43, as:

> "A process that involves overcoming the model of care focussed on the individual, using curative and rehabilitative procedures, to an approach based on the enrolled population, which identifies individuals at risk of becoming ill. It focuses on health promotion and/or preventive action, with early intervention in order to achieve satisfactory results at reduced costs. The management of collective and environmental risks involves surveillance actions (ALMEIDA,p.43,2014)".

Below is a table with examples of quality improvement activities in force in primary care in relation to the principles of clinical governance:

Box 1: Principles of Clinical Governance

Examples of current activities/organisations involved	Strengths	Weaknesses	Opportunities in clinical governance
Quality improvement processes			
Clinical audit led by primary	High levels of	Audit quality needs	Integration with

care groups	professional participation	to be improved	evidence-based practice and continuous professional development (training)
	Improvements in health care	Audit not linked to practice in evidence or professional development	Use of a wider range of method implementations
			Primary care groups for broad clinical data policy
Evidence-based practice, innovative practices, research and development			
Clinical effectiveness not monitored	Improved examples of evidence-based healthcare	Lack of local support e infrastructure	Systematise e manage practice based on evidence through focus groups
	through guidelines or audit protocols		primary
Research networks and individual research practices; university departments		Lack of of training e skills in evidence-based practice	Research practices / research groups
Professional development programmes			
Teaching in hospitals, pharmacies and companies	Groups of self-directed learning	Lack of of management or systematisation	Plan Plan development for multidisciplinary professional practice
Practices based on educational programmes	Clinical supervision (nursing)	Non-needs-based learning	
	Development of Systems for	No é multidisciplinary	

	recertification		
OrcScouiçnec, odvecsos events o clinical risk reduction			
Practice based on procedures of complaint	Resolving complaints locally	Lack of of management or systematisation	Integration with quality, improvement processes, grouping of data at primary care group level
Unsatisfactory clinical performance			
No routine requirement to monitor clinical performance	Clinical supervision (nursing)	Generally not managed or systematised	Actively managing a
			identifying, supporting, and correcting the unsatisfactory performance in individual and team levels.
Professional advice and procedures; health authority	Tool available to monitor and improve performance	Current procedures for extreme cases	Developing occupational health

Source: Own elaboration based on BAKER et al (1999).

In order to guarantee the principles of the ESF, given the changes in the management model, it is important to understand the main aspects of clinical governance in guaranteeing the quality and excellence of the health services offered to users.

Thus, considering the change in the model of care, the process of clinical governance requires well-orientated resources and processes, seeking quality health services, as well as guaranteeing user safety. To this end, it is important that certain principles of clinical governance are guaranteed, such as: support for auditing health care, development and implementation of local guidelines with the participation of users and professionals, continuing education, as well as reliable and consistent technology and information systems to provide effective monitoring and evaluation of health actions (ROSEN, 2000).

According to Baker et al (1999), clinical governance is not an independent process, meaning that the teams responsible for providing health services need to develop important skills and competences to guide health actions with quality and excellence. To this end, the manager must enhance the work of the multi-professional team by encouraging spaces for construction and continuing education that enable professionals to master fields such as information systems, planning, monitoring and evaluation in health, among others that promote continuous improvement in the quality and reliability of the health services offered to the entire population.

Auditing and external support are also important in organising the work process led by the manager. As well as gaining the trust of the team's professionals and a leadership stance to implement clinical governance and assign well-defined functions and roles to the players involved in producing and improving the quality of healthcare actions (ROLAND and BAKER, 1999).

Some examples of actions taken by managers to establish clinical governance are: drawing up a clinic management plan built collectively with the team, planning and defining actions for good clinical governance, a monitoring and evaluation report to be worked on at team meetings, identifying team members' needs for improvement, as well as sources of auditing and support to promote capacity building and training aimed at improving quality and effective methods of good clinical governance. In addition, the manager must be the mediator in this process, acting as a leader and choosing local priorities and needs (ROLAND and BAKER, 1999).

Therefore, responsibility is the key word for good clinical governance. As well as being able to promote improvements in the quality of care, professionals must also demonstrate how and what they are doing, through accountability (ALLEN, 2000).

The great challenge of the current health care model is to break away from medical-centred practices in order to guarantee care based on comprehensiveness and social determinants as the structuring and guiding axis of health practices. Considering user satisfaction and involving them in the production of self-care and the control of issues that affect their quality of life (ASSIS et al, 2010).

CHAPTER 3

Method

This research is an exploratory and predominantly qualitative study that seeks to investigate and characterise the profile of the UBS manager and to learn about the limitations, possibilities and challenges for this professional's work from the perspective of a shared management model.

In order to historically retrieve the concept of managerialism and in what context the position of UBS manager is inserted, a literature review was carried out on these topics, seeking to fulfil the objective of this study.

The review of articles was carried out by consulting the Lilacs and Scielo databases, accessed via the http://regional.bvsalud.org and www.scielo.br websites. These databases were chosen for their ease of access and for being one of the main sources of scientific publications today. The search system used the following keywords: Management, Management of Basic Health Units, Family Health Strategy, Social Organisations. Twenty articles were selected, from 1982 to 2014, as they met the object of this research.

In addition to being a powerful tool for understanding the internal logic of actors, groups and institutions, qualitative research is also a method widely used in studies of relationships, history, beliefs, representations, opinions and perceptions, making it possible to understand how human beings construct their artefacts and themselves (MINAYO, 2013). With this methodological strategy, we sought to identify the specific nature of the work of this professional, who works in a variety of local contexts, with diverse social practices and relationships that are not very standardised.

The study scenario

The city of Rio de Janeiro is divided into 10 health programme areas with 10 Primary Care Coordination Units. The fieldwork was carried out in one area of the municipality, which according to the 2010 Demographic Census has a total population of 886,551 people. Among all the programme areas in the municipality, it is the fifth largest and the third most populous, comprising 14% of the total population of the city of Rio de Janeiro. It is worth noting that some of the neighbourhoods in the selected programme area have a low MHDI, ranking among the lowest in the municipality.

In terms of care models, the municipality's Primary Care units are classified as follows: **Type A units** where the entire territory is covered by Family Health teams; **Mixed or Type B units** where only part of the territory is covered by Family Health and **Type C units** where there is no Family Health team yet, but with a well-defined reference territory (SMS, 2011).

Regarding the classification of the units that had managers participating in the study, 19 units are classified as type A, 03 as type B and none as type C.

The Family Clinics, type A units, have a better quality infrastructure than the Municipal Health Centres, which are older structures, usually adapted as annexes to schools, residents' associations and so on. Considering that infrastructure is an important element in the teams' work process, we decided to select family clinics for the study.

For type B units (where only part of the territory is covered by the ESF), the selection of two units was considered sufficient. These units, located in different neighbourhoods, have specialist professionals as well as family health teams. Type C units, which do not have a family health team, were not included in the study.

Sample selection

This project was approved by the Research Ethics Committee of the Sérgio Arouca National School of Public Health (CEP/ENSP) and the Ethics Committee of the SMS, with opinion numbers 793.484 and 813.007, respectively. In compliance with the basic principles of bioethics described in Resolution 466/12 of the National Health Council, the participants signed an Informed Consent Form (ICF) which clearly and precisely detailed the objectives of the research and its implications.

As a methodological strategy, the 24 questionnaires were sent electronically in Google Docs. The questionnaire was developed by the study's researchers, with the participation of managers and health professionals. Four questionnaires were used in a pilot study with four managers from other UBS.

Of the 24 questionnaires planned for data collection in this study, 22 were answered by UBS managers, representing 92 % of the total. It should be noted that two UBS had two managers each, as recommended by the SMS due to the number of teams. Of the two managers who did not respond, one was on holiday and the other on leave.

Analysis Process

After collecting the data, a statistical analysis was carried out on the results, reporting descriptive statistics such as frequency, mean and standard deviation (SD), which shows how much variation or dispersion there is in relation to the mean. A high standard deviation indicates that there are many discrepancies in the set studied, i.e. many values far from the average.

Frequencies and averages were calculated for the closed questions in the questionnaire. The averages were based on the scores of the answers, considered from one to nine, with the lowest score referring to the answers with the highest priority/importance and 9 referring to those with the lowest priority/importance in relation to the others. In order to discuss the open questions, categories of analysis were chosen based on the content analysis of the managers' reports, according to Bardin's technique (1979). To illustrate some of these reports, the full answers have been included in the discussion of the results.

The topics chosen for analysis based on the questions in the questionnaire were: professional profile, management and work process, care management/clinical governance, the relationship between managers and CAPs and OSs, the main problems/difficulties of managerial work in a UBS, suggested improvements and themes for qualifying/enhancing the work of managers.

The categories used to discuss the results were: professional profile, inclusion in the Family Health Strategy, work management, care management (clinical governance) and managerial role.

For questions in which the managers chose in order of importance, this numbering and standard deviation were averaged. The factors with the lowest averages were considered the most important and the highest averages the least important, and so on. The standard deviation was used to show how close the values were to the average value for each factor assessed. These questions allowed other answers to be inserted if the respondent didn't feel covered by the answers previously described in the questionnaire.

CHAPTER 4

Results and Discussion

Profile of managers

Of the total of 22 managers who answered the questionnaire, 14 are represented by the professional category nurse. Of these, 19 are female, 19 have more than 6 years' training, 13 are aged between 31 and 40 and 3 are over 50, all have some kind of qualification, 5 of whom have a specialisation course in health management. With regard to experience, 14 said they had previous experience in the ESF, 13 of whom had more than 3 years' experience and 5 of whom had more than 4 years' experience.

Table 1 presents the profile of the managers, showing the results discussed in relation to: professional training, gender, time since graduation and age group.

Table 1: Professional Profile

Professional training:	**N**	**%**
Nurse	14	64%
Physiotherapist	1	5%
Biologist	1	5%
Health social worker	1	5%
HR Manager	1	5%
Pharmacist	1	5%
Dentist	2	9%
Nutritionist	1	5%
Total	**22**	100%
Sex	**N**	**%**
Female	19	86%
Male	3	14%
Total	**22**	100%
Time since graduation	**N**	**%**
1 - 5 years	3	14%
6 - 10 years	15	68%
11 - 20 years	2	9%
21 years or older	2	9%
Total	**22**	100%
Age	**N**	**%**
20 - 25 years	1	5%
26 - 30 years	5	23%
31 - 40 years	13	59%
50 years and over	3	14%
Total	**22**	100%
Length of time as a manager	**N**	**%**
Up to 6 months	2	10%
From 6 months to 1 year	1	5%

1 to 2 years	5	24%
3 to 4 years old	8	38%
More than 4 years	5	24%
	21	100%
Previous experience in the ESF	**N**	**%**
Yes, in another municipality	5	23%
Yes, in another Health Unit	9	41%
No previous experience	8	36%
	22	100%

These results point to a predominantly female workforce, with some professional experience considering age, time since graduation and previous professional experience. It can also be seen that the professionals who occupy this position have had postgraduate training in the area of public health, with emphasis on Multiprofessional Residency courses in Family Health (3), Specialisation in Public Health (4), Specialisation in Family Health (3) and Specialisation in Health Management (5), indicating a basic qualification to work in the SUS and the new healthcare model.

Some studies show that even with the trend towards the inclusion of other health professionals in UBS management, there are still cases where this position is held entirely by nurses, as in the municipality of Marília in São Paulo (FRACOLLI and EGRY, 2001).

Ximenes Neto and Sampaio (2007), when studying the municipality of Sobral in Ceará, realised that all the ESF managers included in the study were nurses, demonstrating that this profile prevails because it includes knowledge and practices from the fields of public health, administration and PHC at the heart of their training, and they have been working in the same territory for a longer period of time, which enhances the establishment of links with families and the community.

In this study, there was a trend towards a multidisciplinary profile in terms of professional training. Despite the predominance of nurses, followed by dentists, it is possible to note the presence of other managers from different professional categories: physiotherapist, biologist, social worker, pharmacist, HR manager and nutritionist.

One of the hypotheses regarding the opening up to new professional categories in the management function is a change in the model of care, which points towards more interdisciplinary action guided by the demands of the community from the perspective of health promotion. When it was first set up, the minimum team in the ESF consisted of a doctor, nurse, nursing technician and community health workers. As soon as other professional categories start working alongside the ESF teams, other fields and opportunities for professional development and growth open up, including the management of the UBS.

From the point of view of professional growth, the profile of these new managers is that of a labour force with a longer period of graduation and training.The occupants of these jobs are professionals with a higher age bracket, over 30 years old, with previous experience in other units inside and outside the municipality, which may indicate a turnover of managers between units.

In the study by Ohira, Junior and Nunes (2014), a younger age group was found in relation to these results, where the author relates the demand from young professionals for the position of manager to the prospect that management would be a good career and professional growth option.

With these results, it is possible to hypothesise that the position of manager may be considered a good job option rather than a career option. It is important to emphasise that for these professionals there is no prospect of a career in the public sector or even professional advancement, considering the nature of the contracts and the profile of the contractors. Mobility therefore takes place in the labour market, in search of better pay and professional growth.

In the discussion about the profile of UBS managers in the context of the implementation of the SUS, it's worth drawing attention to a new category that has appeared on the scene of professional training in the area of public health: the Sanitarian. This professional, who has a degree in Public Health, began to be trained in Brazil in 2002 with the first degree course at the State University of Rio Grande do Sul (UERGS). By 2015, there were already 11 programmes at different federal universities, including UFRJ and UFBA. Unlike the biologicist undergraduate programmes of other health courses, which generally seek postgraduate courses to complement their knowledge in the area of public health, public health professionals develop important skills in expanding the needs of the population, management and health care models (ENSP, FIOCRUZ, 2015).

The sanitarian, as a new professional entering the labour market, brings knowledge within a more comprehensive paradigm in the area of collective health, as well as the interdisciplinarity and political character needed to face current challenges, considering that the focus of these professionals' work is in the field of politics, management and planning in the conduct of health services (ANJOS and PINTO).

Although still few in number, the trend is for these professionals to compete in the labour market for this new position or role that is being created in the structure of health services, in the shape of the manager.

The managers' perception of the profile needed to work in this role and the reasons that led them to choose this job point to subjective aspects, such as their identification with the managerial role. They believe they have the profile to work in the position, as well as the political and ideological dimension of believing in the proposal for a new model of care and strengthening the SUS, as exemplified in the managers' reports:

"Because I like management and want to be part of the process of strengthening and expanding the family health strategy. Because I believe that for this to happen, it is necessary to have qualified professionals who understand the principles and ***guidelines that guide the SUS."***

"A challenge in a new area and the chance to collaborate with a system that lacks professionals with a strategic vision."

Management and work process

Of the 22 managers who answered the questionnaire, 10 have between 5 and 8 family health teams under their management. The difference in the number of teams each manager is responsible for can predict a lot about the workload this professional will have to manage. Knowing that a basic health unit has 8 teams, this means that one manager is responsible for more or less 72 team professionals and approximately 32,000 people in the catchment area who should have their access to health services guaranteed.

Table 2: Number of Family Health Teams

Family Health Teams by Management	N	%
More than 8 teams	4	18%
From 5 to 8 teams	10	45%
Up to 2 teams	5	23%
From 2 to 4 teams	3	14%
Total	22	100%

Given the complexity of managerial work, where there is not always a balance in terms of the number of teams coordinated by each manager, as well as the specificities of each territory covered by the UBS teams, personal characteristics such as leadership, autonomy, as well as skills for mediating conflicts and technical knowledge for clinical governance are fundamental for guiding the work of family health teams, within the perspective of managerial work and guaranteeing the principles of the ESF.

Planning is one of the fundamental tools for organising a manager's work. With it, it's possible to map out priorities, prepare for unpredictability and reduce work overload and the discourse that managerial work is based on **"putting out fires".**

When asked about the planning of their activities, 14 managers reported that they sometimes did it, 7 reported that they always did it and 1 manager reported that he didn't do it. As for the spaces used to programme the activities carried out at the BHU, 21 managers said they carried them out at meetings with their managers.

teams, 8 managers from meetings with the CAP and only 5 managers from the OS Coordination.

Even with the work tools available to guide their work, managers have to deal with difficulties and obligations that they are often unable to delegate to others, suffering pressure and having the responsibility of frequently planning and rescheduling their working day.

This professional is in charge of the entire organisation, and is the formal authority that deals with various interpersonal relationships, through which they mobilise information to be used in decision-making and work management (MINTZBERG, 2007).

In the literature, no evidence was found of an established and well-defined work plan, functions and attributions in relation to UBS managers. A document found that was built internally by a group of people from a Social Health Organisation pointed out some of the duties that the manager should carry out in the context of organising a UBS, guaranteeing the principles of the ESF.

As a result, it was possible to identify a certain consensus that this professional should be able to resolve technical and administrative issues, achieving satisfactory results in organising and monitoring the work of the teams, with a leadership stance aimed at improving quality and good clinical governance.

In order to plan the actions developed by the family health teams, managers consider the situational diagnosis of the territory, the epidemiological profile and data from the Primary Care information systems to be essential tools. In view of this, decisions cannot be made randomly. Managers must base their decisions on a systematised process that involves studying the problem based on data collection, producing information, developing proposals and solutions, thus setting the tone for responsible and conscious decision-making, monitoring and subsequent evaluation of the results obtained (GUIMARÃES and ÉVORA, 2004).

Table 8 shows the instruments that managers reported using the most for programming UBS activities.

Table 3: Guiding instruments for programming activities at the UBS

Instruments that guide the activity programme	Average	DP
Data from the Primary Care Information System (SIAB)	2,82	1,40
Ministry of Health regulations	3,18	1,53
Territorial diagnosis, epidemiological profile and population demands	2,09	1,31
Availability of physical space	4,55	1,97
Flows and protocols built locally by family health teams	3,50	1,10
Data from other information systems	4,86	1,08

Even though managers consider information systems to be one of the most important tools for programming activities at the UBS, in practice, the direction of the work often follows a more immediate logic, to meet the demands of the population or more specific actions for the territory.

In this context, the expected results in relation to health indicators need to be monitored and evaluated systematically, safely and reliably by managers, taking into account production, accessibility, quality and efficiency targets (COSTA and SILVA, 2014).

It can be seen that these professionals consider both subjective factors and management tools to be important for the development of managerial work: planning, monitoring and evaluation, the use of information systems/health indicators, leadership and conflict mediation.

Conflict mediation plays a fundamental role in identifying the problem, the players involved, their motives and objectives, providing opportunities for meetings to resolve the conflict and better strategies for dealing with the various situations, so that the conflict becomes an instrument for reflection and transformation of reality (FRANCO, SANTOS and SALGADO, 2011).

The following statements express the perception of some managers in relation to what they believe and consider important for their work:

"The manager must have an understanding and diagnosis of the territory and the network in which his or her health unit is inserted so that he or she can develop the work with the ***team. Tools: Situational Diagnosis, Strategic Planning, AMAQ. "***

"Leadership skills, technical knowledge, organisational and planning skills and conflict mediation. These are characterised as central elements. "

"I think the main thing is to work with data specific to the area. Territorial diagnosis, problematisation, ongoing education. Having a quality information system is essential. As well as knowing and having access to MS manuals and guidelines. "

"Qualification, good relationship with the team, being helpful, being available to professionals, giving constant feedback to the professional on their performance. "

According to Vanderlei and Almeida (2007), managers themselves have different views of their roles. At times, the managerial role is seen as integrative in terms of working relationships, where the team dimension, care and professional performance are valued as the main activities of the job, while at others it is a tougher practice from an administrative point of view, where the main factors considered at work are related to meeting targets, infrastructure and problem-solving.

It should also be noted that the activities listed do not directly cover factors related to clinical governance.

With regard to evaluating the work of managers, the following aspects were highlighted as important in the evaluation process: leadership, planning and teamwork. Other aspects that were not mentioned in the closed answers, but were cited as important for evaluating work, were: interpretation of indicators; knowledge of public policies and knowledge of human resources.

Table 9 shows the most important factors considered by managers when evaluating managerial work.

Table 4: Most important factors for evaluating managerial work

Most important factors for evaluation	Average	DP
Creativity	7,00	2,20
Interpersonal relationships	6,27	1,67
Target fulfilment	6,09	2,18
Meeting deadlines	5,50	2,43
Conflict resolution	5,14	2,62
Initiative / determination	5,05	2,52
Teamwork	4,18	1,79
Leadership	3,41	3,02
Planning / organisation	3,18	2,17

Ciampone and André (2007) draw attention to the fact that the ideas and thoughts expressed and listed in managers' representations are not always materialised in their practices. This leads to a distancing in the way these professionals think and act, which directly influences the operationalisation of health action strategies and consequently the efficiency and effectiveness of managerial work.

This can be seen by analysing the activities that appeared most frequently, which are always carried out as part of the managerial role: planning actions, monitoring and evaluating the work of the teams, liaising with other units in the network, disseminating care protocols, organising and coordinating activities, as well as general UBS meetings.

Another way of analysing the managerial function in a UBS is to use the concepts of structure, process and result pointed out by Donabedian (1980) in the evaluation of health quality. Most managers point out that their functions are related to process: planning, monitoring, evaluating and organising the work process; structure: infrastructure and human resources; and results: achieving targets and aspects of clinical governance.

The excerpts below were taken from the participants' answers and reflect their opinions on the role of managers, considering the categories mentioned above.

*"**Organising the work processes so that the team can achieve the*** objective of meeting the needs of the territory, by evaluating the data provided by the teams themselves. Providing material support through assessments of the ***teams' needs. "***

"To be a facilitator, promoter and stimulator of the work process to be developed by the teams, seeking planning and continuous monitoring, based on the quality of information for the development of ***local*** activities. "

"Ensuring compliance with internal and external flows; providing quality and effective ***access***; encouraging family health teams to plan promotion, prevention, curative and rehabilitation actions; guaranteeing regular supplies; assisting teams in managing the work process; ***promoting the integration of the local network. "***

"I see the manager as a mediator, like a conductor, who must be based on the national primary care policy and its guidelines in the municipality where they work, managing ***manual and intellectual labour with the professionals. "***

The managers' statements reflect a concern with the organisation of the teams' work process, envisaging a managerial role that goes beyond strictly administrative issues. It is possible to identify a perception that the manager must act in a broader way, including intersectoral actions, decision-making and points that favour clinical governance, such as solving flaws in the teams' work process.

Table 10 shows the process, structure and result categories as a way of systematising the managers' statements about the main managerial functions that should be carried out at the UBS.

Table 5: Managers' perception of their role in the UBS

Categories: Structure, Process and Result	N	%
Process: Planning, monitoring and evaluation	11	27%
Process: Leadership	3	7%
Process: Institutional support	4	10%
Process: Clinical governance	4	10%
Process: Organising the work process	6	15%
Process: Conflict mediation	2	5%
Process: Permanent education	1	2%
Results: Information systems/Indicators	1	2%
Structure: Infrastructure and human resources	5	12%
Process: Information systems	1	2%
Process: Intersectorality	2	5%
Outcome: Clinical governance	1	2%
Total	41	100%

Care Management/Clinical Governance

As an example of some actions to establish clinical governance, it is possible to consider the Manager's practice of drawing up a clinic management plan that is built collectively with the team, with planning and definition of actions and goals. Identifying the improvement needs of team members, as well as sources of auditing and support to promote capacity building and training aimed at improving quality and effective methods of good clinical governance (ROLAND and BAKER,1999).

Resources that are well orientated towards guaranteeing good clinical governance, consider user safety and improving the quality of health services through support for auditing health care. In addition, reliable and consistent technology and information systems to provide effective monitoring and evaluation of health actions are still incipient issues in the work process of managers (ROSEN, 2000).

Even so, it is possible to see that some managers understand the importance of improving work aimed at making professionals and users responsible for health production. Thinking about creating spaces for sharing knowledge, defining roles and reducing health risks in a continuous surveillance process.

Table 5 shows the activities prioritised by managers when monitoring the work of their teams, some of which relate to clinical governance/care management. On purpose, few factors related to the topic were included in the closed questions, in order to encourage spontaneity on the part of the managers with regard to the answers that would include aspects related to clinical governance.

Table 5: Most important and prioritised activities in monitoring the work of ***managers and their teams***

Activities	Average	DP
Register all the population covered in the territory	3,27	2,85
Ensure that the teams make a territorial diagnosis of the population they serve	3,68	2,28
Ensuring access to care for spontaneous demand	3,59	2,30
Ensure that users are referred to other levels of care	5,91	1,63
Establish links with the population and social facilities in the area	4,91	2,45
Monitor patient return after external referral	7,50	1,44
Guarantee health promotion actions	6,09	1,95
Stimulate continuing education actions	5,95	2,48
Using information (SIA, SIAB, Indicators) to prioritise health actions in the territory	4,59	2,70

In the open field, where managers could record other important actions for the management of care, only three managers expressed their opinion. They mentioned:

"Stimulate health surveillance, especially of vulnerable families. "

"Ensuring that health professionals are incentivised, through recognition among the teams, for the good work they do. This shows that they are valued and encourages them to improve. In our unit, we have a habit of raffling off prizes to encourage the teams. We've already raffled off one tablet, and we have others in the pipeline. "

"Occcmtir deguimento dos diohas de cuicCodo; doidado com os profissionais; garantir informação de qualidade; estimular resolutividade. "

As described by Baker et al (1999), one of the most important aspects of clinical governance/care management is auditing and user participation, but no response in this sense was directly cited.

This suggests that the principles of clinical governance are still little known in the work process of managers and their teams, i.e. the consolidation of strategies that include the user in the construction of their health is still incipient.

Questions like this carry an important significance, because the perception that clinical governance is part of the manager's work and monitoring process is not spontaneous. This perception follows the logic of traditional administrative principles, where planning is done in a bureaucratic and fragmented way.

Care management is one of the functions most in need of improvement within the managerial function, since the qualification of managers reflects many more aspects of administration than a more comprehensive managerial performance.

Managers' relationship with CAP and OS

One of the most important characteristics for successful management work is the ability to liaise. The interference of more than one actor in management requires commitment and good coordination, especially on the part of the manager, who conducts the work with a view to achieving the best results for the organisation, with the effectiveness and efficiency of the services offered.

This dimension is present in the relationship that organisational actors establish between themselves and with users who take advantage of the services provided. The manager plays a central role in mediating these relationships, because without this commitment to the organisation and its objectives, how will he or she be able to mobilise the other human resources for the organisational task? (JUNQUEIRA and INOJOSA, 1992).

Institutional support, as described by the Paideia method, takes into account the broader concept of management: managerial, political, pedagogical and "therapeutic" functions. In this way, institutional supporters work with the teams, helping them to build collective spaces where the group analyses, defines tasks and draws up intervention projects (CAMPOS, 2003).

With this, the supporter gets involved with the teams in a synergistic, affectionate and propositional relationship, while taking into account guidelines agreed externally to the group, such as: organisational and budgetary directives, political guidelines, programmes, evaluation indicators, as well as reflecting on the interests and needs of the external public (CAMPOS, 2003).

As discussed in the introduction to this study, the concept of Paideia presented by Campos (2003) considers that the managerial function in PHC involves more than a strictly formal and bureaucratic relationship. It is a relationship that involves affection and collectively agreed objectives, in order to guarantee shared management.

From this perspective, in order to carry out his mediating/facilitating role, the manager has to answer to two different social actors: the SMS represented by the CAP and the OSS responsible for providing the contracted services.

In this shared management relationship, the CAP is responsible for guiding the work process and managing care, and the OSS for management, which includes administrative issues, human resources and the achievement of contractual targets.

In this way, establishing harmonious relationships, articulating and directing the manager, considering macro-political issues in decision-making and achieving favourable results are strategies that these professionals have sought in a more autonomous, participatory and shared management (PIERANTONI, 2011; XIMENES NETO and SAMPAIO, 2007).

When analysing the relationship between managers and their superiors, it is essential to discuss the aspects involved and the role of each institutional actor in the work dynamic.

Of the 22 managers, although 17 recognised CAP and OSS as their direct managers, 4 considered only CAP and 1 manager only OSS, suggesting that there is no clarity as to the institutional role of these different actors.

This duality is completed when analysing the answers about institutional support, where 13 managers considered CAP and OSS as their institutional support, 7 only the OS and 2 only CAP.

It seems that CAP and OSS take different stances when providing institutional support to UBS managers. If there is an understanding that shared management depends on joint construction and monitoring of actions, institutional support takes place in a democratic way, but it is often confused with verticalised management, where only demands are made without the commitment/involvement of the parties, culminating in low effectiveness and resoluteness of the desired results.

Without the establishment of a horizontal relationship between supporters and managers/teams, within deliberative spaces, there is a risk that shared management will be blocked by the creation of expectations that generate dangerous relationship patterns that threaten the whole constructive process. However, knowledge of this movement becomes an important management resource for critical analysis and the development of skills that better direct actions and the dynamics of this management space between different actors.

The lack of a clear definition of roles leaves it up to management alone to liaise between the different players and teams, placing greater responsibility on one party and potentially jeopardising management.

Reports reinforce the differentiation perceived by the managers in relation to the different actors and their way of participating, varying between institutional support aimed at the work process and other support aimed at demanding results.

onV OS works closely with me, meeting demands and supporting the organisation. This is not the

case with the other institutions (CAP, SMS and others). "

"The OSS is more resolutive and responds promptly to issues when presented. "

Main problems/difficulties of managerial work in a UBS

Managers report external problems and difficulties such as territorial violence, unachievable targets and users' lack of knowledge about the services offered at the UBS. Internal problems include motivation, professional qualifications, work overload and institutional support.

This scenario draws attention to the autonomy and role of the manager in relation to clinical governance. Given that faced with so many problems, these professionals feel powerless and fail to develop their potential in relation to clinic management issues.

Below are some of the statements that highlight the anxieties and anxieties of those who are institutionally responsible for the results of the UBS:

"Managing a team with a large number of medical certificates, requiring direct support from the company's HR/PD team. In addition to the high turnover of professionals due to the location of the unit and a violent territory that sometimes ***makes it impossible to work in the field. "***

"Unfortunately we've come across professionals who aren't committed to the job they do and are very reluctant when we propose changes. We know that financial matters are important, but love and dedication for what we have chosen as a profession is unfortunately less and less visible in professionals. ***There is a lack of commitment, availability and ethics (respect for different types of knowledge). "***

"Infrastructure, conflict management and keeping professionals motivated in the working conditions in which we operate. "

"I believe that the greatest difficulty is dealing with the demands requested (spreadsheets and courses) by the OS and CAP that must be answered immediately, which crosses the planning of the day/week/month. "

"oteopelamente conétprio. Many domapdor, many poizop. Everything is a priority. People are faced with huge and multiple demands in very short timeframes. Support is lacking. Instruments are lacking. Training is lacking. Valorisation is lacking."

"PoaOadhar aoo apoflppioaaip aeoqoaldfwadstt; aooco support from management in relation to the qualification of the profpippionaip; many political/party interventions. "

"To be able to motivate THE professional in the face of serious problems with the unit's structure, increasing episodes of territorial violence and targets that don't take the local reality into account. I believe that the same targets (regardless of the unit's structure) are an obstacle to the work of units like the one I manage, because they are unattainable due to our reality. "

Suggestions and themes for qualifying/enhancing the work of managers

The testimonies of the managers presented below regarding the qualification and potentialisation of their work emphasise the need for greater investment in training. They also address issues of administrative autonomy, collective spaces for sharing experiences and discussing problems, as well as greater psychological support.

"It would be interesting to provide a management course for managers, as UNASUS already does for the ESF. "

"Encouragement for professional development such as: Master's degree, courses in the areas of People Management, Strategic Planning, Conflict Management, HR... "

"Payment for performance; monthly budget for purchases based on specific needs; support for an MBA in management or other management course; continuing education "

"Monthly workshops between managers and institutional/territorial supporters of the nearest units with themes within the lines of care with discussions/exchanges of experiences for the qualification of care in the SUS. "

"Improvement in the number of employees (faster hiring) and financial resources under the responsibility of the Management (e.g. revolving fund). Autonomy in maintaining our Unit's infrastructure. "

"I believe that there is still a need for greater clarity about the role of each level of management (local management, cap, oss). "

"Greater emphasis and valorisation of the qualification of professionals, with permanent

education actions, routinely and not just on a one-off basis. "

"I would like to receive more (institutional) incentives for my professional technical qualification. "

"I think that if the secretariat, together with the OS and CAP, had a model of care aimed at managers, in a "group therapy" format, where professionals from a multidisciplinary team would work on relieving tension or stress, through conversation circles where managers would have the opportunity to talk about their anxieties and fears, or even to open up without fear of being misinterpreted, this would motivate us much more, to return to the unit with a new gas in order to be truly motivating for our teams. What I miss in our day-to-day lives is having this time to ourselves. With professional help to keep our mind, soul and body in balance. In other words, I miss a Caring for those who care project for managers!!! "

The managers' reports show that there is a real and legitimate need to listen and share their anxieties and issues related to the obstacles of managerial work. The proposals include: creating spaces for managers to exchange experiences; developing competences/skills such as qualified listening, leadership, autonomy, clinical governance, people management; conflict mediation; shared, participatory and democratic management; planning, monitoring and evaluation based on information systems and health indicators.

User satisfaction and the quality of the services offered are also important points, but they are rarely mentioned by managers and should be included in possible specialisations or training aimed at improving managerial work.

Qualification processes for the work of managers are still incipient in the reality of UBS management. Studies such as Ohira, Junior and Nunes (2014) show that although the participants had experience as managers, more than 70 per cent of them had not taken any management courses or training. This scenario leads to the conclusion that there is a lack of professionalisation, training and institutionalisation of the position of manager.

On the other hand, as Junqueira and Inojosa (1992) point out, the skills and competences needed to deal with the problems and difficulties inherent in the managerial role do not depend solely on training in how to be a manager. It is necessary to develop and improve technical and administrative skills in professional practice, liaising with all the players and sharing management in a democratic way.

As part of this, institutional support for shared management, in addition to continuing education processes, must include issues such as conflict mediation, people management and strategic planning. Above all, they must consider the manager as a coordinator and articulator of the network and of clinical governance processes based on protocols and improving the quality of the services offered to users.

CHAPTER 5

Final considerations

The aim of the research was to investigate the limits, possibilities and challenges of the work of Basic Health Unit managers in the context of shared management between the state and a social organisation in the municipality of Rio de Janeiro. The results point to the strategic importance of this professional as a fundamental element in the process of implementing and strengthening Primary Health Care.

Based on the results presented, we identified critical issues to be worked on prospectively in order to strengthen and qualify the performance of this function, which was the subject of our investigation, namely: competences; selection process; qualification; clinical governance and shared management.

The first question that arises when analysing the work process of managers, both in the literature and in their reports, is the lack of a clear definition of the managerial role in the UBS.

While in the National Primary Care Policy the duties of the professionals in the family health teams are well defined, in the case of the managerial role in the UBS there is no single work guideline or document that formalises the main duties of the managers. This can make it difficult for managers to plan and organise their activities, and for managers to establish criteria for selecting, monitoring and evaluating the work of these professionals.

The definition of the managerial profile, functions, competences and the establishment of a selection process with specific notices, norms and criteria that take into account the qualifications and skills needed to perform the job are fundamental issues for the functioning of the UBS. The weakness of this process in the current model can jeopardise the entire logic of the work, as well as the monitoring of the teams' health actions.

In the analysis of the work process, it became clear that the practice was geared towards more bureaucratic processes, with a focus on productivity, but with gaps for reception and the user as the centre of health production. These difficulties, combined with other complexities such as power disputes and the inhibition of professional autonomy, can hinder a more humanised practice, leading to a hegemonic managerial rationality.

It is important to institutionalise the process of permanent education, deconstructing plastered and ultra-specialised practices, promoting greater autonomy on the part of professionals and users in the production of health with constant monitoring and evaluation.

With regard to clinical governance, what can be seen is that, suffocated by administrative demands, care management, despite appearing in the words of some managers in an unsystematised way, is not highlighted in the day-to-day activities reported.

Adopting clinical governance as an axis for the qualification and continuing education process can be an effective strategy for strengthening teams and technically directing the work of managers.

In addition, the challenge of shared management must be considered in its internal dimension - managers and teams - and in its institutional dimension - CAP, OS and labour management. The complexities of a system with actors from different levels of power (CAP and OS) influence and put pressure on labour management.

The results found point to work overload, present in many reports, in addition to the diversity of professionals' thoughts, the multiplicity of tasks to be carried out at the same time and the inability to control the course of their work. In this context, managers report difficulties, as they are overloaded with obligations that they often cannot delegate, they are under pressure and frequently have to plan and reschedule their working day.

Finally, we believe that the proposals listed here, as well as the institutionalisation of the position of UBS manager, with policies and guidelines to guide their work, are elements that induce the teams to work more effectively in PHC, transforming the current reality and strengthening the ESF.

Bibliographical references

ABRUCIO, F.L. and SANO, H. Promises and results of the new public management in Brazil: the case of Social Health Organisations in São Paulo. **RAE- Revista de Administração de Empresas**, v.48, n. 3, 2008.

ALLEN, P. Clinical governance in primary care: Accountability for clinical governance: developing collective responsibility for quality in primary care. **BMJ,** 321:608-11, 2000.

ALMEIDA, P.F. **Mapping and analysing Primary Health Care models in South American countries.** Authoritative document on PHC in South American countries. South American Institute of Government in Health-ISAGS, 2014.

ANJOS, D.S.O. e PINTO, I.C.M. **A Formação de um novo Sanitarista: expectativas para inserção no Mercado de Trabalho.** Centre for Research in Social Sciences- CICS-Publications/eBooks. University of Minho. Available at: http://www.lasics.uminho.pt/ojs/index.php/cics_ebooks/article/view/1908. Accessed on 13 October 2014.

ASSIS, M.M.A., et al. **Production of care in the Family Health Programme: analytical views in different scenarios**. Salvador: EDUFBA, 2010. 180 p.

BAKER, R.; et al. A model for clinical governance in primary care groups. **BMJ,** 318:779-83, 1999.

BRAZIL. MINISTRY OF HEALTH. **Basic Operational Standard for the Single Health System**. Brasília: National Health Council, 1996.

BRAZIL. MINISTRY OF FEDERAL ADMINISTRATION AND STATE REFORM. State Reform

Chamber. Masterplan for the reform of the state apparatus. Brasilia: MARE; 1995. Available at: http://www.bresserpereira.org.br/documents/mare/planodiretor/planodiretor.pdf. Accessed on 19.02.14.

BRAZIL. MINISTRY OF FEDERAL ADMINISTRATION AND STATE REFORM. **Reform of the state apparatus and constitutional changes: summary and answers to common questions.** Brasília: Ministry of Federal Administration and State Reform, 23p.,1997.

BRAZIL. MINISTRY OF HEALTH. **Manual for the organisation of primary care.** 3. ed. Brasília: Ministry of Health, 1998.

BRAZIL. MINISTRY OF HEALTH. **Operational guidelines for the Pacts for Life, in Defence of the SUS and Management.**1. ed. Brasília: Ministry of Health, 2006a.

BRAZIL. MINISTRY OF HEALTH. **National Primary Care Policy.** Brasília: Ministry of Health, 2006b.

BRAZIL. MINISTRY OF HEALTH. **Primary Care and Health Promotion**. Brasília: Conselho Nacional de Secretários de Saúde-CONASS, 232 p. (Coleção Progestores - Para entender a gestão do SUS, 8), 2007.

BRAZIL. MINISTRY OF HEALTH. ORDINANCE NO. 2.488, OF 21 OCTOBER 2011. **Approves the National Primary Care Policy, establishing revised guidelines and standards for the organisation of Primary Care, the Family Health Strategy (ESF) and the Community Health Agents Programme (PACS).** Legislation - GM (PNAB), 2011.

CAMPOS, G.W.S. PAIDÉIA AND MANAGEMENT: An essay on Paideia Support in the workplace in health, 2001-2003.Available at: https://www.dropbox.com/home/SA%C3%9ADE%20COLETIVA%20UNICAMP/Gest%C3%A3o%20and%20Planning?preview=APOIO+PAID%C3%89IA.pdf. Accessed on: 24 February 2015.

CAMPOS, G.W.S. Efeito Paidéia e o campo da saúde: reflexões sobre a relação entre o sujeito e o mundo da vida. **Trabalho, Educação e Saúde,** v. 4 n. 1, p. 19-31, 2006.

CIAMPONE, M.H.T e ANDRÉ, A.M. Competências para a gestão de Unidades Básicas de Saúde: percepção do gestor. **Rev Esc Enferm**. USP, 41(Esp):835-40, 2007.

COSTA e SILVA, V. **Third sector and partnerships in health: Social Organisations as possibilities and limits in the management of the Family Health Strategy**. Thesis presented to obtain the degree of Doctor of Science in Public Health. ENSP/FIOCRUZ,2014.

DONABEDIAN. **Quality in the local management of health services and actions**. Health and Citizenship. Book 03. Available at: .http://www.saude.sc.gov.br/gestores/sala de leitura/saude e cidadania/ed 03/03 05.h tml. Accessed on 12 February 2014.

DUARTE, I.G. and BOTAZZO, C. People management in Social Health Organisations: some observations. **Revista de Administração em Saúde-RAS**, Vol. 11, n. 45, 2009.

DUSSAULT, G.A. Management of public health services: characteristics and requirements. **Rev. Admin. Púb.**, Rio de Janeiro, 26 (2):8-19, 1992.

ESCOREL S. et al. The Family Health Programme and the construction of a new model for primary care in Brazil. **Rev. Panam. Salud Publica**, Washington, v. 21, n. 2-3, p.164-176, 2007.

ESCOVAL, A.; SILVA, V.C. and HORTALE, V.A. Contractualisation in Primary Health Care: the experience of Portugal and Brazil. **Rev. Ciência & Saúde Coletiva**. 19(8):3593-3604, 2014.

FERREIRA, A.S. Competências gerencias para unidades básicas do Sistema Único de Saúde. **Rev. Ciência & Saúde Coletiva**, 9(1):69-76, 2004.

FRACOLLI, L.A. and EGRY, E.Y.. Management work process: a powerful tool for operating in health practices? **Rev.Latino-am Enfermagem**; 9(5): 13-8, 2001.

FRANCO, T.B. e JÚNIOR, H.M.M. **Integralidade na assistência à saúde: a organização das linhas do cuidado**. In: MERHY, E.E. et al. Trabalho em Saúde: olhando e experienciando o SUS no cotidiano. 3. ed. São Paulo: Hucitec, p. 125-133, 2003.

FRANCO, C.M; SANTOS, S.A. e SALGADO, M.F. **Desafios da média gerência na saúde.** Manual do Gerente: Instituto de Comunicação e Informação Científica e Tecnológica em Saúde/ Biblioteca de Saúde Pública, Rio de Janeiro, National School of Public Health ENSP/FIOCRUZ, p.208, 2011.

GAULEJAC, V. Gestão como doença social: ideologia, poder gerencialista e fragmentação social. Editora Idéias letras.3ª edição. P.107-153, 2007.

GIOVANELLA, L. et al. Family health: limits and possibilities for a comprehensive approach to primary health care in Brazil. **Ciênc. Saúde Coletiva,** vol.14, n.3, p. 783-794, 2009.

GONÇALVES, J.B.B.; BARBOSA, P.D. e SOUZA, R.R.M. Qualidade da assistência em saúde da família: uma breve reflexão. **Revista Funec Científica** - Multidisciplinar, Santa Fé do Sul (SP), v. 2, n. 3, 2012.

GIDDENS, A. **The Third Way and its critics.** Rio de Janeiro. Record, 2001. Translation by Ryta Vinagre.

GRAU, N.C. **Accountability for social control. In: CLAD. La responsabilización en la nueva gestión pública latinoamericana.** Buenos Aires: Eudeba, pp. 269-327, 2000.

GRIGOLETTO, M.V.D. e RAMOS, L.H.D. **Gestão de serviços de saúde.** Open University of the SUS-UNASUS. Collection of educational resources in health, 2012. Available at:< http://ares.unasus.gov.br/acervo/handle/ARES/178>. Accessed on 13 February 2014.

GUIMARÃES, E.M.P. and ÉVORA, Y.D.M. Sistema de informação: instrumento para tomada de decisão no exercício da gerência. **Information Science**. Brasília, 33(1), p.72-80, 2004.

JUNQUEIRA, L.A.P. Gerência dos serviços de saúde. **Caderno de Saúde Pública**, RJ, 6 (3): 247-259, 1990.

JUNQUEIRA, L.A.P. and INOJOSA, R.M. Gestão dos serviços públicos de saúde: Em busca de uma lógica da eficácia. **Rev. Adm. Púb.**, Rio de Janeiro, 26 (:2): 20-31, 1992.

LIMA, S. M. L.; RIVERA, F. J. U. Contractualisation in Teaching Hospitals in the Brazilian Unified Health System. **Ciênc. saúde coletiva**. Rio de Janeiro, v. 17, n. 9, p.

2507-2521,2012. Available at <http://www.scielo.br/scielo.php?script=sci_arttext&pid=S141381232012000900031&lng=pt&nrm=iso>. Accessed on:16 April 2015.

Law No. 9.637 of 15 May 1998. **Provides for the qualification of entities as social organisations, the creation of the National Publicisation Programme, the extinction of the bodies and entities it mentions and the absorption of their activities by social organisations, and makes other provisions.** Presidency of the Republic, Civil House. Brasilia, 1998.

Law No. 5.026 of 19 May 2009. **Provides for the qualification of entities as Social Organisations and makes other provisions. Municipality of Rio de Janeiro, 2009.**

LOCH, S. **Becoming a manager: the experience lived by family and community doctors when they took over the management of basic health units.** Doctoral thesis. Submitted on 18 December to the Federal University of Santa Catarina, Postgraduate Programme in Production Engineering, 2009.

MACHADO, R.R. et al. Understanding the pact for health in SUS management and reflecting on its implementation. **Rev. Eletr. Enf.** 11(1):181-7, 2009.

MAFFEI, S. **The creation of the position of manager in the Family Health Strategy: the case of the Municipality of Rio de Janeiro**. Monograph presented as a final paper for the Specialisation Course in Public Health at the National School of Public Health/ENSP-FIOCRUZ, 2011.

MARTINS, H. F. Política de Gestão Pública no Governo Lula: um campo ainda fragmentado. **Revista Eletrônica sobre Reforma do Estado**, Salvador, n°5, March/April/May, 2006.

MERHY E.E. and ONOCKO R. **Acting in health: a challenge for the public**. São Paulo: HUCITEC; 1997.

MESQUITA; D.T.; MOREIRA; A.C.A. and XIMENES NETO, F.R.G. Manager job satisfaction in the Family Health Strategy. **Revista de Administração em Saúde-RAS**, Vol. 15, n.59, 2013.

MINTZBERG, H. **The maiiager's job: folklore and fact.** In: VECCHIO, Robert P. (editor). Leadersship: understanding the dynamics of power and influence in organisations. 2. ed. University Notre Dame Press, Notre Dame Indiana, 2007.

MOTTA, P. R. **Gestão contemporânea: a ciência e a arte de ser dirigente**. 7. ed. Rio de Janeiro: Record, 1996.

MINAYO, M.C.S. Contradictions and consensuses in the combination of quantitative and qualitative methods. In: Minayo, M.C.S. (Ed.). **The challenge of knowledge**. São Paulo. Hucitec, 2013. P. 54-76.

OHIRA, R.H.F.; JUNIOR, L.C. and NUNES, E.F.P.A. Profile of Primary Health Care managers in small municipalities in northern Paraná, Brazil. **Ciência & Saúde Coletiva**, 19(2): 393-400, 2014.

PASSOS, J.P. e CIOSAK, S.I. A concepção dos enfermeiros no processo gerencial em Unidade Básica de Saúde**. Rev Esc Enferm**. USP; 40(4):464-8, 2006.

PAULANI, LM. **The neoliberal project for Brazilian society: its dynamics and impasses.** In: Lima, JCF; Neves, MLW (org.) Fundamentos da educação escolar do Brasil contemporâneo. Rio de Janeiro: Editora Fiocruz/EPSJV, 2006, p. 67-108.

PINTO, E.G. **Plano diretor da reforma do aparelho do estado e organizações sociais. A discussion of the presuppositions of the "model" for reforming the Brazilian state**. 2001. Available at: http://jus.com.br/imprimir/2168. Accessed on 01 January 2014.

RAMIRES E.P., LOURENÇÃO L.G. e SANTOS M.R. Gerenciamento em Unidades Básicas de Saúde: conhecendo experiências. **Arq Ciênc Saúde**, 11(4):205-9, 2004.

Final report final of the **Brazilian Association of Postgraduate Studies in Collective Health-Abrasco** on Graduation in Collective Health. **IX Brazilian Congress of Collective Health**. Recife, 29 to 31 October 2009. Available at:< https://saudecoletiva.wordpress.com/2010/07/05/relatorio-fmal- abrasco/>. Accessed on 10 January 2015.

REZENDE, C.A.P. **O modelo de gestão do SUS e as ameaças do projeto neoliberal.** Updated text. Opinion of the National Health Council Working Group. Debate on Bill 08/2003, 2004.

RODRIGUES, M.G.M. **Articulação entre sociedade civil e setor público estatal: mudanças na área da saúde após a década de 80**. Master's dissertation presented to the Sergio Arouca National School of Public Health. ENSP/FIOCRUZ, 2007.

ROLAND, M. and BAKER, R. Clinical Governance: a practical guide for primary care teams. **National Primary Care Research & Development Centre**, 1999.

ROSEN, R. Clinical governance in primary care: Improving quality in the changing world of primary care, **BMJ**, 321:551-4, 2000.

SILVA, V.M. **Social Organisations (OS) and State Private Law Foundations (FEDP) in the Unified Health System: aspects of the public-private relationship and control mechanisms.** Dissertation presented to obtain the title of Master of Science in Public Health. ENSP/FIOCRUZ, 2012.

STEWART, R. **A model for understanding managerial jobs and behaviour**. Academy of Management Review. v. 7, n. 1. p. 7-13, 1982.

VANDERLEI, M.I.G E ALMEIDA, M.C.P. A concepção e prática dos gestores e gestores da estratégia de saúde da família. **Rev Ciência & Saúde Coletiva**, 12(2):443- 453, 2007.

XIMENES NETO, F.R.G. and SAMPAIO J.J.C. Territory managers in the Family Health Strategy: analysis and profile of qualification needs. **Rev Bras Enferm**. 60(6): 687-95, 2007.

ZALEZNIK, A. **Management of disappointment. Managers as leaders**. A Harvard Business Review Paperback. Boston (MA): Harvard Business School Press, 1993.

ZWANENBERG, T.V.; HARRISON, J. Clinical Governance in Primary Care. Oxon UK, Second Edition, **Radcliffe Medical Press,** p. 253, 2009.

Printed by Books on Demand GmbH, Norderstedt / Germany